FIRST LIGHT:
Five Plays for the Very Young
By Matt Bassett and Tia Shearer Bassett

Cover Art by
Jess Breznai of Bagels N Pretzels Illustration

LICENSING & PRODUCTION INQUIRIES
Uproar Theatrics, LLC.
hello@uproartheatrics.com I www.UproarTheatrics.com

Table of Contents

<u>**Nutt and Bolt**</u>
A Nonverbal Play for Ages 2-6
by Matt Bassett

CHARACTERS:

Nutt, a robot – Nutt is a junky, jangly collection of spare parts. He communicates through percussion and plosives, banging and clanging in both joy and displeasure. Nutt is gregarious and outgoing, sometimes going a bit too far in vocalization or physicality. Nutt does not trust his electric neighbor, mostly because he's jealous of Bolt's quickness and sleekness, so he keeps Bolt at a distance and makes every effort to outdo Bolt to prove his own relevance. And Nutt just can't make heads or tails of that beeping…

Bolt, a robot – Bolt is a quick, slick electronic entity. She communicates through bleeps, bloops and whistles, which can show her joy in quick, bright tones or displeasure in shrill or somber tones. Bolt is friendly, yet unsure of just how to make friends. Bolt is exasperated by her clunky, yet interesting neighbor who would certainly get along with Bolt just fine if Nutt would stop being so loud, clangy and bangy. Bolt tries to show Nutt how to do things THE RIGHT WAY, but Nutt just wants to mess things up!! And Bolt just can't seem to understand all that banging…

NOTES FROM THE PLAYWRIGHT:

Characters are listed as he/she, but please note any actor can play either role and the more gender-fluid characterization can be kept, the better. - While the through-line of the story is set, specific beats can be discovered by individual production teams. The initial production followed an aesthetic of using only found objects, which served it quite well in personalizing character. This draft will provide examples to spark the imagination, but I encourage you to let your team develop NUTT and BOLT, their voices, and their world as you will. It's more fun that way, anyway!

SETTING:
A junkyard. NUTT and BOLT's lean-to-like areas face each other from opposite ends of the playing space. The audience surrounds them in alley-style staging. NUTT's home is a ramshackle collection of found objects, strewn about much like a young child's room might be that loves each thing they possess with all their heart, but is easily pulled away to the next thing before they can put those beloved toys/books/ clothes where they came from. BOLT's home is orderly and neat, each well-loved piece exactly where it should be, much like the child that finds comfort in stability, organization and knowing where something is exactly when needed. A uniformity of pieces is encouraged, as if BOLT is part of a set, in contrast to NUTT's cobbled-together feel.

<u>I: Who's This?</u>

The audience enters to NUTT and BOLT playing games and building small structures. Each makes their way around the space, making new friends as they go. NUTT clanks and clangs, stacking pieces into fun towers with audience members that they knock down together. BOLT zips and floats about, inviting the audience to press buttons and create sounds, sliding other pieces together into orderly patterns and structures. Actors are invited to develop other games with the audience.

At curtain, BOLT disappears into her home. NUTT introduces himself to the audience, showing off lots of fun noisemakers and other assorted junk strewn about his ramshackle, yet well-loved home. This is an excellent opportunity for audience participation in making sound, looking/speaking across the playing space to other kids, or pretend play (going to work, cooking, etc.). In his play, NUTT accidentally creates a mess in BOLT's orderly area. He quickly and quietly (and messily) covers up the mess, then exits to dig up something really cool to show his new friends. Loud beeping startles NUTT before he can re-enter. He hides as his obnoxious neighbor makes an appearance.

BOLT enters shortly after, introducing herself by floating around the playing space, gleefully beeping for the audience and showing off her various buttons and keys (in the initial production, BOLT's body included a child's keyboard, with microphone, on its torso, as well as a small synthesizer and a harmonica, all pieces allowing for lots of musical/sound/beat opportunities), making sound and playing music as well as engaging in similar audience participation and pretend play as NUTT. In her intro, BOLT finds NUTT's mess and straightens up. For good measure,

BOLT straightens up a particularly messy area in NUTT's home as well.

This brings NUTT out of hiding and ready to face off with BOLT. They bang, clang, beep and boop at each other before stomping/floating away. They face off, each in a corner that serves as their home, surrounded by objects, and decide to compete for the audience's favor.

II: Sound-Off

NUTT and BOLT engage in a contest of sounds to impress the audience. In the initial production, this included for NUTT: playing a simple melody on a makeshift cigar box guitar, clanging on a makeshift triangle, and a very special object: in this case, a door chime, making two clear, clean tones that make NUTT very happy.

For BOLT, initial production choices were: a snippet of Tchaikovsky's *Nutcracker Suite* on their keyboard body, a button with laser sounds, and a found bell.

The sounds themselves can be made of whatever actors are attracted to/whatever the production team creates, but the through line is that BOLT counters every sound NUTT produces with something cleaner, flashier and easier to reproduce. When BOLT counters NUTT's extra-special small sound with something almost identical, yet more efficient and clean, NUTT explodes into loud, aggressive sound (initial production team created this with videocassette cases filled with beans). This causes BOLT to emit her ugliest sound yet, just to get some peace and quiet.

III: Dance-Off

With NUTT temporarily abashed by BOLT's outburst, BOLT shows off another feature of her cool body by pressing a button that starts a looped beat, possibly with a melody (in initial production, BOLT's keyboard included a "demo song" feature, which made this section quite fun for kids and adults who recognized the songs the robots dance to). BOLT then starts a crisp, simple dance – the Robot, of course! – that involves small, precise angular movements in the arms and torso.

NUTT scoffs and takes over BOLT's beat and the space with his own version of the Robot, using his segmented, ramshackle body to bring an impressive range of articulation and flexibility to the dance floor. This should evoke images of wheels spinning, cranks turning, and levers pulling. (In the initial production, this gave us a fun opportunity to invite the audience into a group dance with NUTT that engaged bi-lateral movement).

BOLT, embarrassed at being outshone, hits a button that speeds up the rhythm, sending NUTT careening around the space and, ultimately, to the ground in a heap. BOLT cannot help but laugh and gloat a bit.

IV: Building the Tallest Tower

Frustrated and more than a little embarrassed, NUTT decides to just ignore BOLT and build. NUTT's not sure what he's building, but he knows it's one thing he is really good at that BOLT cannot ruin. NUTT clanks and clunks together a foundation of loose parts and starts to enjoy simply building a tower. A tall, tall tower. There's no way BOLT can mess that up.

BOLT sees this – a tower!! BOLT can totally build a tower, too!! But so much easier and stronger by smoothly slotting and sliding pieces in just so, making it perfect. This will show that jangly sourpuss that BOLT actually knows a thing or two!

BOLT calls NUTT's attention to the new tower and is met with derision. It's not nearly as tall as NUTT's. BOLT, who was definitely not looking for a contest, is now more than happy to give NUTT a run for his money. BOLT brings out more pieces from her home and constructs an intricate tower of many pieces, elegantly placed to be juuuuust tall enough to beat NUTT, which BOLT only too happily shares with her neighbor.

The pair then engage in placing one piece more on their respective tower at a time, with maximum showrobotship to engage the audience. NUTT, building from frustration, ultimately collapses his tower in a heap. BOLT celebrates her victory (in the initial production, this was a "ta-da" from BOLT's harmonica). NUTT responds by pulling one piece from the base of BOLT's tower, sending the whole thing crashing down. This sends both robots into a fierce argument.

V: Fight

NUTT and BOLT argue, a fury of beeps and clangs, whistles and sputters. This escalates into an all-out war of sounds, with each robot making the loudest sound to drown out the other. Finally, a sound of BOLT's (in the initial production, a button that produced a loud siren and red flashing light) overwhelms NUTT, who balls up on the ground and covers his ears, breathing deeply to try and self-soothe. BOLT beeps with concern - that wasn't supposed to happen and she realizes she went too far. BOLT moves away to give NUTT space to recover. Perhaps after a check-in with the audience, BOLT unearths a small, simple object that produces a small, simple sound to soothe NUTT (in the initial production, this was the small bell BOLT used earlier in the sound contest). The sound breaks through NUTT's anxiety, drawing his attention. BOLT then finds a way to speak to NUTT in percussive notes (this was a function on BOLT's keyboard torso in the initial production, but could be created through foley). NUTT responds, truly surprised to hear his own language spoken. BOLT carefully approaches NUTT and offers the simple object, which NUTT gratefully accepts.

VI. Sharing and Transformation

NUTT answers BOLT's gift with a gift of his own: a noisemaker clipped from NUTT's own body! (A horn in the initial production). After playing with it, BOLT offers the object back, but NUTT won't have it, finding a hook on the sleek robot's torso to clip onto. Now BOLT looks a little bit like NUTT! Delighted, BOLT pulls a piece off herself to offer in return (in the initial production, the laser button from earlier in the show) and sticks it to NUTT's ramshackle body. Now NUTT looks a little like BOLT! The robots then switch other pieces (goggles and a hat in the initial production), until they look more and more like two new, mixed entities. They find a reflective surface to admire their new looks and, inspired, move around the space experimenting with new movement and sounds: beep/clangs, jaunty walks and floating. Finally, they are able to talk and listen to each other!

VII: Building Together

NUTT builds an orderly tower while playing as "Bolt." When BOLT goes to knock it down, both robots stop to admire how cool their building pieces look together. After a short conversation of beeps, clangs, notes and whistles, the two robots construct, together, their tallest, most elaborate (yet intricate) structure yet, using pieces pulled from both of their homes. The hybrid structure, constructed from NUTT's spare parts and BOLT's uniform blocks and jars, fits together beautifully, showcasing what the two can accomplish together. Colors blend and highlight each other, shapes mingle and dance within the structure. The robots take in what they've made, pointing out especially cool parts to each other and the audience, before topping it with the first gift exchanged between them and high fiving/beeping/clanging/however-you-want-to-celebrate in triumph!

VIII. Music Together

NUTT and BOLT celebrate their new project by making sounds using their bodies. BOLT jangles any pieces hanging off of NUTT, NUTT presses buttons on BOLT. This leads to a rhythm, found in the initial production through a preset key on BOLT's body. Further experimentation finds BOLT able to mimic the simple melody sung/played by NUTT earlier in the show, but this time in electronic notes. NUTT is delighted - BOLT can jam! The robots dance and sing together, engaging the audience through clapping, shakers, singing in "beeps and boops." (In the initial production, this included NUTT building a drum kit out of spare parts to accompany BOLT and the audience). The music crescendos with everyone - robots, children, parents/caregivers - contributing to the song in their own way. The robots bring the group to a big finish and congratulate each other and all their new friends.

IX. Goodbye?

A signal arises (a light shift? A whistle? Up to you!) that reminds the robots that it's time to go back home and recharge. NUTT hesitantly offers a hand to BOLT, who is surprised by the direct contact and awkwardly shakes. They turn and, a little sad, make their way home.

NUTT makes it a few steps before signaling BOLT with the initial gift (a bell in the initial production). BOLT turns, unsure of what new game is about to start. NUTT offers a simple invitation. "Want to come over and play at my house?" (Translated from the percussive Nuttese, of course.) BOLT happily beeps and whirs her way over to NUTT's messy yard, overcoming immense discomfort at the possibility of stepping on/in something, to find a seat has been put together and cleaned off by a nervous, yet excited host.

NUTT cobbles together an instrument and, with BOLT's help, tunes up. BOLT, strict at first about tuning up exactly right, relaxes and enjoys the sound they make together, in tune or not.

NUTT and BOLT sit together, quietly playing their song, admiring the tower they built, enjoying the ways in which they differ, yet are the same, as the play ends.

<u>**Out of the Box**</u>
A Nonverbal Play for Ages 1 ½ -5
By Tia Shearer Bassett and Matt Bassett

CHARACTERS:

PJ, a child (played by an adult) – PJ is adventurous, warm, and wide-open to the audience. Although the performer is alone(ish) onstage, <u>PJ</u> is surrounded by friends – the BASS, her stuffies, and the audience. Her first impulse with each discovery, each new box and the adventure inside, is to share it. Avoid impulses of performance, however, as PJ herself's arc involves abandoning a "performance" and instead choosing to explore possibility with her friends.

BASS, a musician/companion – So, this doesn't *have* to be an upright bass, but in creating the piece, we found it useful for the following elements:
- Size – a big instrument provides a great visual contrast with both PJ and the three stuffies.
- Sound – the upright bass allows for an expressive voice, good percussion, and (when a bow was briefly used) surprising beauty.
- Prop/set – stuffies and PJ can use a bass to play hide and seek, PJ could jump off the sturdiest part of it, and it provides helpful weight for things like anchoring tight ropes. All of that said, if an option exists for your production that serves those needs and isn't an upright bass, GREAT. What's important about BASS is that the instrument and player are a warm, playful, slightly more mature presence to counter PJ (think Hobbes of Calvin and Hobbes).

STUFFIES, preferably custom made for the show – these are PJ's best friends. They follow her through her adventures, get lost, play tricks, and sometimes propel PJ forward. They do not need to be manipulated to "move" in anything but the simplest ways – they don't walk or talk, they are clearly stuffed friends animated by PJ, but they have the reality invested by imagination. There are 3 stuffies at 3 levels:
- Big – this one is stable and excited to be playing.
- Middle – this one can be the tallest, as long as they are still able to be considered "Middle" in relative size. This stuffie is not always sure about things, but game nonetheless.
- Little - clearly the smallest of the three. Watch out for this one, they're always just short of trouble.

NOTES FROM THE PLAYWRIGHTS:

With some ingenuity, you can truly pull off this show with a series of cardboard boxes. We used basic size comparisons, and our production designer was able to rig a box that opened only when tapped twice. Maybe yours is able to unfold into a cave or has built-in boat attachments that get revealed. Have fun, get crafty!

SETTING:
PJ's playroom. It can be sparse or decorated. All it needs is room for the BASS to live, room for PJ to move, and easy access to the audience to share in the magic.

I: A Game of Magic

We begin with our young heroine, PJ, attempting to amaze the audience with a magic show! She has a top hat and a cape, and manages to pull three differently-sized stuffed animals "from nowhere" (though perhaps the audience sees her hide a critter in her hat before theatrically pulling it out). She bows after each trick, presenting each new critter in turn, then introduces her friend and musical accompanist, the BASS. Thinking that her imaginary game is over, PJ turns to leave...only to discover a **new thing** (perhaps brought on by our stage manager while PJ and BASS greeted the audience). *Note for box-reveal: In the initial production, the box is the table upon which PJ performs her magic show and is revealed when, in a final flourish, PJ whips the cloth from the table. At this point, the box is "announced" with a music cue from BASS with PJ in appropriate awe or PJ ignores the box until BASS calls her attention to it himself.*

PJ stands, holding her three best friends (who happen to be stuffed, but a friend's a friend, no matter what they're made of) and eyeing this new thing with a mixture of trepidation and excitement - a little more of the latter than the former. As she stands, her companion, the BASS, encourages her to explore. BASS is a guiding voice for PJ, keeping her out of trouble and getting her into it whenever she most needs him. At BASS's urging, PJ moves to the object, which we know is a large cardboard box.

II: What's This?

PJ is a thorough young lady, so she investigates the box completely, engaging sight, sound, touch and taste (fact: cardboard boxes do not taste very good). When she's satisfied her scientific curiosity about the box's exterior, she follows BASS's suggestion to pull the string on the box's top to open it. Not sure what to expect, she pulls the string and then zooms away, hiding behind (or on top of!) BASS until given the all-clear.

Once open, the box offers a whole new mystery: What's inside? After sending a stuffed buddy or two on reconnaissance, PJ peers into the box herself, then dives in completely! She rummages, eliciting a questioning strain from BASS, before she emerges with her bounty: another, smaller box!

III: Littlemiddlebig

This new box yields yet another box, which yields a fourth, each successively smaller, like nested dolls (if one's idea of a doll was square and brown). PJ lays these haphazardly next to each other, but notices something's not quite right. She lays each buddy by a box and sees that they don't quite match. PJ rearranges the boxes into an order of descending size, each with a corresponding buddy. PJ has the idea to place a buddy on top of a box, which elicits a note from BASS. PJ notices that BASS makes a note for each buddy on each box and that each note is different, with higher pitches for smaller boxes and lower pitches for larger boxes. She then conducts a short piece with BASS using stuffed buddies as a baton. Finally, PJ herself hops onto the largest box, eliciting the deepest note of all!

IV: Making Sounds and Music

PJ returns to drumming briefly, until she hears a rattle come from one of the smaller boxes. PJ turns all her attention to this box and its new mystery. She hesitates for a half second only before diving into the box, legs kicking in the air! BASS asks what she's finding, until he finally can't take the suspense and peers as far as he can from his place to see what PJ sees. Just as he gets a view, something flies out of the box, making BASS jump! PJ's head emerges next, as she looks for whatever she just dislodged from inside the box. After a little looking, helped by BASS, she finds what she pulled from the box: a small cardboard tube!! "huh?"

PJ examines this new thing. It can be anything she wants it to be! It's a sword, it's a baseball bat, it's a pole vault pole for her littlest buddy. It's a tool to use to tickle the BASS! But when she puts it to her lips and makes a sound, she finds out something new entirely when BASS answers her noise. PJ makes another noise, which BASS repeats. PJ makes a noise into the audience to see if they can do it, too. The noises range from highpitched hoots to low bleats. This call-and-response game among BASS, PJ and the audience slides up and down the BASS's neck, letting PJ and BASS explore all the parts of a musical scale with the audience until the game turns to music. BASS takes the lead, moving PJ and the audience to connect noises into notes, then into melody. BASS and PJ join forces to lead us into a jam around our play's main musical theme. The jam ends with PJ and BASS teaching the kids around them to play the song through instruments made out of their own hands and mouths!

V: Newspaper Ocean

PJ dives back into the largest box and notices a strange noise under her feet. She digs her toes into the box and enjoys the sound and the feel of what she's standing on. She reaches down to the bottom of the box, feels around and comes up with a wad of newspaper! She plays with the

newspaper and notices it makes a special kind of sound
when she waves it around, which gives her an idea. She
hops out of the box and runs over to the BASS. She slides
the bit of paper through the BASS's strings, which gives him
a fun new voice. They play with this new voice, with BASS
playing and PJ dancing.

Once PJ puts one of her buddies into a smaller
box and dances around with it, BASS begins a sea chanty,
which gives PJ a whole new idea! PJ leaves her buddy in his
box and dives back into the larger box. We hear a rustle of
newspaper, then PJ pops back up wearing a newspaper
captain's hat! She waves, salutes, then dives back in. More
rustling, then PJ reappears with a tiny newspaper captain's
hat for her buddy! She puts the hat on the buddy, he waves
and salutes, then PJ and BASS play with the sea chanty and
the boat as she situates her other two buddies behind the
captain.

This is good, but PJ realizes we need something
more to complete the image. She dives into the largest box
one more time, rustles among the newspaper, then emerges
with a strip of newspaper that turns out to be very long
indeed. She examines the piece briefly, looks at us and puts
two and two together. PJ launches into the audience,
stringing the long piece of newspaper around to as many
kids as possible. After a brief moment to show the kids and
parents how to make the newspaper sound like rolling
waves, PJ runs back to the boat and the BASS, ready to take
to the sea!

<u>VI: Picnic on the Other Side of the World</u>

As PJ of the Waves, our heroine sails her buddies
over the newspaper ocean of the audience; around, over and

through the kids she sails them, until, finally, the little boat comes to rest behind the audience. PJ brings the boat to land and leaves her buddies to collect the newspaper ocean from our kids and helpful grownups. With the newspaper, PJ returns to her buddies and lays the newspaper out in front of them. She takes the buddies out of the boat and arranges them on the newspaper for a picnic on this new little island she's found! PJ and her buddies eat and drink, sharing with any audience member that wants to join and noticing that she wants to share with the BASS, who finds himself alone on the other side of the audience.

PJ wants to make her way back to BASS, who is indeed quite lonely on the other side of the audience, but how? She thinks and thinks until she notices a sea of helpful hands between her and BASS. She shows the audience how to float her box of buddies back to the other side like waves in the sea. She swims ahead through the audience to meet her buddies on the shore. PJ is a good sea captain, arrrrh!

VII: A Secret Cave

Once back "home," PJ begins to straighten up the place, gathering up newspaper and dropping it back into the biggest box. Littlest Buddy wants to help, so he sticks with her. She moves to the box to replace the newspaper and notices something at the box's bottom. She looks to the BASS, who shrugs "I don't know, go see."

PJ reaches into the box, but doesn't seem to hit bottom. She reaches further, her arm up to the shoulder, but still finds empty air. She stands and bends over the box, sending her whole upper body into the box. Still nothing! With a courageous wave to BASS, buddies and audience, PJ climbs over the side and lowers herself into the box. We hear her voice as she descends deeper and deeper down what sounds like a deep well. BASS calls to her. She answers, but as if from very far away. BASS tries to move over to see her, but he's stuck where he is.

We hear a shriek of victory from deep within the box, and then something flies out of it. It's a net! It lands near BASS, who quickly secures it with his bottom - bottoms come in handy sometimes! We hear PJ climb up the walls of the cave before she emerges, victorious and clutching something. Once she reaches solid ground, she thanks BASS for the assist and the audience for cheering her on before examining this new thing she found in the cave - the smallest box yet!

<u>VIII: Something is Wrong...</u>

PJ turns her attention to this new smallest box, which is closed. She pushes it, hearing a rattle. What's making the rattle? PJ shakes the box, tastes the box, yells at the box, but cannot figure out what's in this new box! And then something dawns on her. She runs to her buddies and counts: 1...2...WHERE IS LITTLEST BUDDY?! She searches everywhere (Is he under this purse? Is he in that child's hands?) until finally the audience indicates the box-cave. Oh no! PJ kisses her remaining buddies and puts them in the care of a trustworthy grown-up or two (she is not taking any chances now!). Then she bravely and dramatically descends into the cave one more.

She is gone for longer this time, and the box is silent and still. BASS starts to get visibly worried. Suddenly, there is a little shake. And then another. And then...Littlest Buddy appears, climbing up and out of the box cave followed by PJ. BASS is relieved and delighted as PJ and

Littlest embrace. She gratefully gathers Middle and Big for a group-hug around/with BASS. All is right in the world. Now BASS can gently remind PJ of the current mystery: the smallest box.

IX: Fabric and Transformation

She brings it to the BASS and the two examine the box for any seams. She brings it to her circle of buddies, and sits bewildered for a beat when Middle Buddy simply pats the top of the box. Then Big Buddy pats it. Then Littlest. So PJ pats it, too. And then she brings it 'round to the audience, thinking perhaps the power of all these hands might do the trick (like loosening the lid on your peanut butter or jelly). BASS gets the final pat, and then--perhaps with a drum-roll flourish--the tiny box magically OPENS, revealing a sliver of white fabric!

PJ reaches for the fabric and gently pulls it out, but finds more fabric. She pulls more, but still finds no end! PJ then rolls up her sleeves, tugs with all her might and comes up with the longest piece of fabric she's ever seen! PJ uses the fabric to dance, costume herself and decorate her largest box (and maybe the BASS!)

After playing with the fabric's BIGness, PJ balls it up again and attempts to squish it back into the tiny box, with little success. Some part of the fluffy ball is always sticking out! She tries to pat it down, which is when she realizes...it is very soft. Pleasant! Reminds her of something...she pats a nearby buddy's head, then returns to patting the fabric. Delighted, she pulls the rolled-up fabric out of the box and cradles it in her arms like a kitty. She even makes kitty noises for it. "Meow, meow!" as she pets her new friend. She invites the audience to meow (or something

18

similar) with her as she brings the "kitten" around to her little friends and their grownups for petting. Perhaps the kitten squirms a bit or cuddles up to certain lucky people. She leaves the kitten in the trusty watch of her three buddies when...

X: Tightropes and Puppet Shows

PJ notices the string she tossed off from the big box. It lies on the floor, just begging to be played with. Perhaps one end of it is still stuck under the big box. She pulls it taut and steps on it. A tightrope! BASS sounds his note(s) of caution, and PJ searches for the netting she found earlier. She places it under her tightrope. Perfect! BASS turns the atmosphere into a circus as our young acrobat balances across her imagined highwire, arms out. She makes it to the other side! Now, for her next trick...she gathers all 3 of her buddies and crosses while balancing the stuffed pile in her arms. After a wobbly but definite triumph, all 4 take a bow. PJ invites BASS to bow, too!

All this excitement can make a pal long for home. PJ sees this in her buddies and starts to clean up, gathering the netting and the string, when another idea strikes her. She puts the net away but continues holding the string in the air...she proceeds to make a clothesline going from the big box to a pillar in the room, or down to the bottom of the BASS. But "home" is difficult to get into with the door at the top! She tips the big box over, then adjusts her clothesline and begins to stick stuff up on it with the clothespins she found in another box. With a cozy home set up, Peej is ready to put her buddies down for a nap. She gathers them around her and rocks Littlest Buddy while she urges BASS to play a lullaby. One by one, she sets her sleepy little charges in the Box-home. Napping seems underway (lullaby and all) when...Littlest Buddy peeks out from the box!

Littlest Buddy takes a look around at the audience, then dashes back into the "house" after being gently berated by Mama PJ. Littlest Buddy's foot peeks out from the box, takes a look around at the audience, then dashes back into the house. It is clear who our story's comedian is! PJ heads into the box to coax him back to sleep, but Littlest proceeds to play peek-a-boo up and down the box's opening. Perhaps he even makes it to the top of a flap and sits up there on the ledge for a while before performing some impressive acrobatics down. Eventually, the other buddies in the box get restless and catch on. Middle's arm appears; Big's head pops out! And eventually-eventually, PJ's foot!

After the group puppet show, PJ is ready to clean up. She picks up the smallest box--now, she thinks, empty.

XI: Magic

But still, the smallest box rattles. PJ looks and looks, but cannot find the last piece of the box until she turns it upside down, shakes it hard as she can and dislodges a little light the flies around the room! We then see PJ chase the light through the audience, where it might stop and hover for the audience to touch it themselves. Finally, PJ catches the little light and puts it into the smallest box where the fabric and it came from.

Now it really is time to tidy up and call it a day. PJ and BASS make a quick game of building a tower of boxes and buddies, all tucked in by the fabric. Once PJ is sure that her buddies are snuggled in and ready for a nap, she yawns, stretches and bids us goodbye. On her way offstage, she stops to flick off the light switch, at BASS's reminder - got to save electricity!

Once PJ is clear, BASS bids us adieu with a magical strain that… changes things. Suddenly, the floor directly beneath the sleeping buddies begins to glow. Lights, like the one PJ just chased, arise beneath the stuffed buddies! We're left with that image for a moment before BASS brings his person downstage to take a bow, then calling out for PJ to join him!

* * * * *

__Magic Post-Script:__ During the show, the lobby of the performance space has been simply but completely transformed. The lighting should be different; perhaps the floor is different (i.e., the children and their grown-ups have a path to walk on now). The idea is that the magic of the final scene--the new colored light; the explosion of stars - has seeped out into the lobby, following the audience out the door, and, with any luck, well beyond.

<u>Space-Bop</u>
A Nonverbal Play for Ages 0-2
By Tia Shearer Bassett

CHARACTERS:

Simone (or Simon) – a gentle clown, curious and calm. Chaplinesque in costuming and style. While much that happens in the play is surprising to our quiet clown, she is not one for showy emotionality. She is quite affected by the world, don't get me wrong…but she is definitely an adult, and a rather even-keeled and grounded one at that. Her sense of humor and sense of play come through in a twinkle in the eyes, a small smile, deliberate and soft gestures. When she sets her mind to creating a spacecraft to bring a wayward star home, she does so with focus and determination and know-how. (It is the circumstances I've written for her that are absurd. She herself is generous, reasonable and self-assured despite the strangeness of the world.)

CracklePop – a musician and beat-boxer. Think of CracklePop as…the live scoring we all secretly wish we had in our lives. Well, Simone actually DOES have it! CracklePop should have their own little setup where they stay for the whole show, but they can engage with Simone in little ways throughout the show (and this is sometimes written into the text). BIG NOTE: This role was written for a beat-boxer in the original production. That said, there are other forms of live musicality and soundscape that could work! The important things are:

-the sounds of "real" space should be different and surprising for the audience as well as Simone. Perhaps more staccato/rhythmic than the melodic music of S's everyday life.

-we should be able to watch CracklePop create the music and sounds live, before our eyes.

Both of these characters are any age, any gender, and pure big-hearted playfulness.

SETTING:

A tent or giant multi-blankie fort, big enough to fit the audience.

Perhaps a coat rack in the space. Audience on all sides?

A Reminder: To engage this littlest of audiences as much as possible, find moments to bring objects and experiences right up to them! Gentle offerings to touch things, objects flying sweetly or goofily over little heads, sounds that grownups are encouraged to mimic to their kiddos, sounds that come from the kiddos themselves that can be mimicked by a performer or puppet. Work to weave each group of babies into the fabric of this world!

<u>I: Pre-show</u>

The audience is gently, playfully introduced to the space, characters and soundscape.

-C is already in the space as audience enters, engaging them in some beatbox repetition.

-Music shifts when S enters (from hip-hop to sweet, playful ukulele), home from a long day of work.

-S takes in the audience, the musician. Is only mildly surprised to find all these beings in her "house."

-S joins the audience to watch the musical performance but starts to think she is supposed to be part of it instead…she joins C as best she can sans instrument (and, well, rhythm. And coolness….)

- The show officially begins as S settles in for the night….

<u>II: Making Space</u>

S & C turn the tent into a homemade cosmos.

-Having tucked herself into bed, S is bored. Absently plays with flashlight beam against wall of tent (perhaps there are some poor attempts at shadow puppetry)…

-C makes the beam sound like a shooting star! This is awesome! Together, with just sounds & the flashlight, they make stars streak across the walls and ceiling.

-The flashlight gets S's attention and pulls her out of bed to discover a glowing orb hidden right there in her room! S, amazed and delighted, shares the orb with the audience. She places it up to her ear and discovers it has a song (provided by C). Jams out briefly before hanging the orb above the audience.

-S uncovers two more orbs, smaller than the first, and plays with them together, finding they too each have their own music (and a whole new song when listened to simultaneously)!

-Satisfied, she sits back on her bed to enjoy fake outer-space when…

III: Space Invasion!!

"Real" space enters the scene, in the form of a new little pal.

-C makes an altogether new sound! And from this sound comes, crashing into the room…a real Star!

-Summoning bravery (with C's help), S approaches the glowing object to examine it and the space around it. Whenever S looks away, Star comes briefly to beatboxing life, only to hush when S looks back. Finally…

-Star comes to life ("voiced" & puppeted by S with sound effects by C), and begins zipping around the room, clearly calling/looking for someone.

-The Lazzi of Containing the Zooming Star! (Star pulls S around the room, exploring the children, searching but often sidetracked. She zooms around S's neck and shoulders, tickling her, before pulling her up onto a height to indicate that she needs to get back to outer space.)

IV: A Giant Leap…

S. decides to boldly go where no clown has gone before.

-S tests the aerodynamics of various objects before C gives her beatboxed instructions on building a rocket

-S grabs some material and begins furiously mime-sewing, sawing, etc (accompanied by either correct or mismatched sounds from C)…in a "ta-da!" bait-and-switch moment, a rocket made out of that exact fabric is revealed!

-S fastens Star to her and they journey together into space!

V: The Funny Frontier

By way of a wee Astronaut, S. explores other planets.

-(NOTE: "Real" space should be an entirely different soundscape! This is a world of beatboxing and different instruments than were played with in parts I-IV. Also, "real" outer space should involve more twinkly lights, but not yet all of them.)

-S lands the spaceship on a hospitable surface (perhaps after a few failed attempts – a grownup's head? A baby's foot?)

-A tiny astronaut puppet emerges from the rocket!

-S & Astronaut float through space, exploring. Two different bouncy balls/orbs get sent into the tent from outside, one at a time. Each "planet" has its own distinct sound and feel – Planet One is slow and pleasant. Astronaut hitches a ride on it across the children. Planet Two is a quick, shaky planet! Astronaut attempts a ride, but keeps getting bounced off!

VI: Beatboxin' in the Rain

In which an old standard gets a cool & cosmic reimagining.

-Astronaut needs a break after all that rigorous adventuring, so S drops him off at the spaceship.

-Star is clearly sad and searching for someone when – by way of C's sounds and S's head indicating the movements she is   seeing - a meteor shower strikes! C gives them an umbrella to hide under, prompting a hip-hop "Singin' in the Rain" dance number between S & Star. Star has fun but hides afterward, still upset about something...

VII: Awe

S. goes night-swimming in the wake of a beautiful creature.

-…a comet creature enters the space. This is a creature that moves in a wholly different way – the atmosphere changes with her crossing. She seems to be underwater.

-S watches her in wonder. She floats about the space and around the audience, clearly calling/looking for someone… she approaches C, who points her in the direction of…

-her lost little Star! They reunite joyfully, and the three of them (S, Comet and Star) "swim" together for a lovely moment.

-Comet swims off. Star follows, but not before turning back and "thanking" S in her way. S thanks her uniquely too, and waves good-bye as she disappears.

VIII: Going Home

-S is alone.

-She pulls out a jar and scoops a bit of "space" into it as a memento.

-She returns to the rocket and flies it backward to get home.

-At home: S is alone.…

-S is…alone. It is quiet. She doesn't know what to do with herself.

-With C's nudging, she remembers and pulls out the jar of stars. She unscrews the lid and her whole tent home is suddenly and wonderfully flooded with stars.

She is not alone at all.

She has brought the magic of the universe home with her.

<u>**Under the Canopy**</u>
A Nonverbal Play for Ages 0-2
By Tia Shearer Bassett and Matt Bassett

BRIEF SYNOPSIS: The rainforest wakes up, one creature at a time.

PRODUCTION NOTES: This play was produced in collaboration with Wit's End puppets, who collaborated with directors and actors to generate puppets for each character. The puppets generated not only reflected the desired visuals to evoke a living rainforest, but also involved shapes, colors, sounds, and textures to enrich the youngest audiences. We encourage play and joy over realism.

For puppeteers, we encourage walking a fine line between keeping the puppets alive and the audience engaged while not engaging in character (the puppets, rather than the puppeteers, are the story's characters). Fill the puppets with life via movement, voice, and focus. Move to a new puppet to aid it in "waking up" to discover the audience or each other. We found vocal, but nonverbal internal lives for the characters worked best. A simple, repeatable pattern of voice or instrumentation engages the babies well and helps them develop pattern recognition. We found percussion instruments, flutes, kazoos, and other noisemakers a great complement to the vocal choices of puppeteers.

For the set-up, three ladders are placed in a triangle formation with plenty of room between. There is a stump in the center, and audience on 2 sides of the triangle opposite each other.

After each "character's" small story, the set should be a bit transformed – a bit more of the colorful rainforest is exposed. And each little story should lead to the next in a gentle relay between characters.

This piece was originally performed with a soundscape playing the entire time – actual rainforest birds/sounds mingled with the recorded vocalizations of the playwrights' son at 3, 6 and 9 months old! While the parents and caregivers didn't seem to notice, we swear there were babies who would perk up at a sudden baby chirp amid the avian chatter….

<u>I: Pre-show</u>

The audience is gently, playfully introduced to our world.

- Actors play with chosen objects, audience, and each other, and end by adding their objects to the environment (i.e. adorning a ladder with extra flowers and branches).

- End with focus on Ladder 1. (Perhaps a bell is rung on that ladder? A bell is one of the early sounds a baby will turn toward!)

<u>II: Flower Discovery</u>

A flower finds her voice…and height!

- Actor 1 discovers a flower at the top of Ladder 1. She puppets the flower while Actor 2, from afar, must find the right sounds to make the flower grow upwards (as opposed to side-to-side or in a rotation, as this tricky flower is wont to do)!

- End with kazoo buzzing, leading to…

<u>III: Butterfly and Bee</u>

A butterfly begins to form as a bee makes its rounds.

- Actor 2 discovers a bee in the center stump. Actor 1 creates a butterfly out of dowels at Ladder 1. They meet at Ladder 3, where butterfly "lands" and one of her dowels gets attached to bee by Actor 1.

- Bee continues to explore the space while Actor 2 watches. Bee checks out the musical flower, checks out Actor 2, makes way back to Ladder 3 and disrupts a gourd (held/manipulated by Actor 2) at the top!

- Gourd comes swinging down, dangling from our ladder tree. Finding this a bit unsettling…bee settles.

- End with focus on gourd at Ladder 3. Both actors there.

IV: Caterpillar

A caterpillar ventures through the space to butterfly-hood.

- Gourd swings around the ladder before being "caught" by Actor 1 (who had been punctuating gourd's movements with sound)…

- Caterpillar awakes! Actor 1 puppeteers (and voices) his gourd-exit and subsequent journey; Actor 2 provides his inching sound.

- Caterpillar's journey: down Ladder 3 (with vine attached to his bum) – inching/flipping across floor to Ladder 1 – up Ladder 1 – swings on vine to land near base of Ladder 2 – up Ladder 2 (here, Actor 2 secures vine to make tightrope) – partway across tightrope, where a particularly daredevil maneuver (a hanging spin?) causes the butter-flower at the center stump to pop up via Actor 2!

- Caterpillar climbs aboard the flower and they become a lovely Cloth Butterfly, taking a spin over the audience (via Actor 2) before settling down on Ladder 2.

- Her settling awakens Umbrella-Bird!! (Actor 1 and Actor 2 together – 1 as front of bird, 2 as umbrella tail)

V: Bird

A celebration-prone umbrella-bird gathers colorful bits for her nest.

- Umbrella-Bird thinks the world was draped in color just for her! She finds scraps at Ladder 1 – brings them to center stump – at Ladder 2 – brings them to center stump, then adds her wing-"feathers" to the pile as Actor 2 folds her umbrella tail into the trapdoor of the center stump.

- The idea behind Umbrella-Bird's elegant dismantling is: we go from the actor bodies creating Bird to the Bird being simply the umbrella tail, now tucking down into her nest.

- End with actors kneeling or seated on either side of stump, facing nearest audience.

<u>VI: Frogs</u>

Two Puckish frogs raise havoc!

- Actors begin by making their particular frog sounds to the audience.

- The frogs come out of hiding! Each actor gets one, and they visit different sides of the audience until one of them discovers the "nest" (pile of cloth scraps) on the center stump. Calls to the other one, and they make a gleeful mess of it.

- They part again, until one discovers the tightrope. They play on and over it…until it comes to life as a giant snake! (Actor 2 takes both frogs; Actor 1 unties the tightrope from Ladder 2 and puppeteers the vine-snake).

- Snake tickles them and chases them to Ladder 1, where they settle. Snake visits some audience until…Spider-Guy appears!

<u>VII: Spider</u>

An affable spider-guy journeys to the center of the world.

- Actor 2 brings Spider-Guy out from hiding on Ladder 1 – Spider-Guy reaches out and tickles the snake, sending it to rest on Ladder 3.

- Actors team up to walk Spider-Guy around. (Spider-Guy should not move like a realistic spider does.)

Spider-Guy occasionally reaches an arm or two out to play with the audience, or wave from afar. He makes his way to the center stump. For him, it is…

- A trampoline! He bounces for a while until he realizes he is on top of a door. He opens it, and Umbrella-Bird (now just umbrella and sound, via Actor 1) flies out!

- Umbrella-Bird flies around the space, taking Spider-Guy for a quick spin!, before perching on top of Ladder 2. Spider-Guy lands near the base of Ladder 1, where he discovers a huge flower! He plucks it and offers it to Actor 1. She receives the gift and places it in her "vase" (the open stump, where there is a base to secure the stalk).

- Spider-Guy reaches into the open stump/nest and pulls out "eggs" (egg shakers) for a group egg-shaking moment, creating the sound of rain as…

VIII: Canopy

Our little rainforest is completed.

- The audience is encouraged to continue the egg-shaker rain as real rain sounds are heard in the space. Spider-Guy comes to rest hugging the stump like a big brilliant flower. The actors retrieve three swaths of canopy – one fastened to the top of each ladder, hidden in plain sight – and connect them to the upright flower in the center stump.

- Once the canopy has been raised, the actors sit or kneel around the stump, quietly taking it all in.... then they look to the audience with an invitation.

IX: Exploration

The world is handed over to the children.

- The little ones and their caregivers are invited to explore the space and its objects! After stowing the more fragile items, the actors help facilitate play.

****

<u>**Outside the Lines**</u>
A Nonverbal Play for Ages 2-5
By Tia Shearer Bassett
*Possibly – but not necessarily - produced with the help of
artful projection design,
and tango music.*

Characters - Two pen-pals:

Vi (female-presenting)

Bud (male-presenting)

Physical Life

She moves through space and time as if there were a lot of both.

Her topography (path across the floor, the earth) is full of fat, lovely, inefficient curves.

It's how they do things, where she lives. It is what's expected.

Her body, however, is at constant odds with this - gestures of straight lines abound. Or rather, her gestures do whatever they wish.

He moves through space and time as if they are in short supply.

His topography (path across the floor, the earth) is a grid of straight lines and sudden turns.

It's how they do things, where he lives. It is what's expected.

His body, however, is at constant odds with this - soft, curvy gestures abound. Or rather, his gestures do whatever they wish.

Until, that is....

***

Early morning.

Vi and Bud are asleep in their separate locations, but both in little tents within their houses.

A pile of lines rests above each of their heads.

Curvy lines for Vi, straight lines for Bud.

She stirs, and the curvy lines spring into action to make her world:

> *Soft, curvy house, quiet street, rolly rolly hills.*

He stirs, and the straight lines shuffle about to make his world:

Straight-line house, noisy street, tall tall buildings.

They both wake up, and begin different but simultaneous morning routines. A parallel tango of sorts.

A moment of sleeping (shared snores?)

"Alarms" (he pops awake, she fights it)

Still in bed: he reads for a bit. She finds and gnaws

yesterday's apple.

They fold their [quite different] blankets.

They arise,

brush teeth,

spit and mirror-check.

She checks her mailbox, he gets an envelope tossed at him. It is mail from the other! They each receive a self-portrait the other has made.

They hang them up by/on their tents and wave hello to them.

They sit down to write a silly thank-you.

They send these letters and…

Mail instantly received! They open and read their thanks from the other.

It makes them laugh.

They capture the laugh and send it to the other.

(At least one of these laughs is a bit unruly – the envelope flips, flops and flutters about!)

Mail again! …for Vi. This time, Bud has to wait. (He is not great at waiting.)

She opens the envelope and Bud's laughter moves through her space.

Mail for Bud, at last!

He opens the envelope and Vi's laughter moves through his space.

Meanwhile, Vi has sat down to the day's work: making flowers from a pile of curvy lines.

Bud sits down to his own day's work - making bowties from a pile of straight lines – as Vi gets an idea…

She stuffs some curvy lines into an envelope; sends it.

She continues working.

Mail for Bud! He receives it instantly, and pulls curvy lines out of the envelope [that perhaps he already had].

SO MANY FEELINGS.

He loves them. He moves with them. He remembers he is not "allowed" to love or move with them. He shoves them back into the envelope, and sets it down away from him.

He stuffs some straight lines into an envelope; sends it.

He continues working.

Mail for Vi! She receives it instantly, and pulls straight lines out of the envelope.

SHE DID NOT EXPECT THIS. She loves them. She moves with them. She remembers she is not "allowed" to love or move with them. She shoves them back into the envelope.

They each now hide these envelopes.

They change their minds and retrieve them.

They change their minds again and put the envelopes under their pillows.

Simultaneous bedtime routines –

fast-forward and reverse of morning routines!

Afterward: settled in their tents.

They carefully retrieve the pillow-envelopes and have a loving moment…but, NO, CAN'T!

They thrust the envelopes outside their tents.

They shove their heads under their pillows.

But the lines are stirring…

And they whip up into a STORM.

The storm brings them together.

They recognize the other. (It is wonderful. It is overwhelming. It is newness and familiarity in a tango with each other.)

This storm-space (this dream-space) is neither of their houses but feels most like home, because something key does not exist here: expectation.

Vi moves like VI.

She moves to and around him in straight lines, here, but

throws in a curve whenever she feels it.

Bud moves like BUD.

He moves to and around her in curves, here, but throws in

a straight line whenever it suits him.

They have never done this before.

They did not know they could.

But they are certain that it is only possible because they are now together…

Except that the storm subsides.

It puts them back to sleep and deposits them back in their tents.

They wake up.

…

…

LOSS.

They each try to mail themselves to the other, putting stamps on their tents and curling up inside…

But it doesn't work.

They each go to those certain envelopes.

Dump them out. Fiddle with these new-but-familiar lines. Get an idea.

They move to their workspaces.

He adds curvy lines to one of his bowties as

She adds straight lines to one of her flowers.

The result is the same, and they each hold up

A flower bowtie.

(…or a bowtie flower.)

She fastens hers to the center of her collar while he wears his off to the side.

But both wear them [so, so] proudly.

A reminder that they know who they are, and that someone else knows, too.

A reminder that there is ROOM out there for their expansive selves. The world can hold them.

It can hold all of us.

***